RETIREMENT READINESS

Creating Your Vision, Knowing Your Position,
& Preparing for Your Future

RETIREMENT READINESS

Creating Your Vision, Knowing Your Position,
& Preparing for Your Future

By Mike Bonacorsi CFP®

PETER E. RANDALL PUBLISHER LLC
Portsmouth, New Hampshire 03802
2008

ISBN10: 1-931807-71-5

ISBN13: 978-1-931807-71-5

Library of Congress Control Number: 2008928336

Published by:
Peter E. Randall Publisher LLC
PO Box 4726
Portsmouth NH 03802
www.perpublisher.com

Book design:
Grace Peirce

Cover cartoon:
Bob Nilson

Additional copies available from:
www.mikebonacorsi.com

Contents

Preface vii

Introduction ix

Chapter 1: See Your Future 1
Dream a Dream

Chapter 2: Create a Plan 12
Lay the Groundwork

Chapter 3: Take Inventory 28
Look at Money

Chapter 4: Bumps in the Road 61
Prepare for the Unexpected

Chapter 5: Make Sure It Goes Where You Want It to Go. . . 75
Prepare Your Estate

Chapter 6: Now That I Have Your Attention. 92
Go for It

About the Author 94

Preface

I decided to write this book to make you aware that the same attention you give to planning for retirement must continue during retirement.

I believe everyone needs to create a retirement vision, assess the situation, and prepare for any bumps in the road before leaving a regular nine-to-five. This preparation will allow you to follow your dreams into the next life stage, and should begin before you start life in retirement.

Maybe it's because I'm a boomer myself that I'm paying more attention to the idea of retirement readiness. I remember when my grandfather left the mills in Lawrence, Massachusetts. He retired at sixty-five and lived to sixty-nine. Retirement for him was short and uneventful. Now, my friends and clients are getting ready to retire and are talking about a completely new world awaiting them. Before they get there, however, they need to get ready.

Introduction

This is not a book about a great investment strategy, a hot new product, or a guarantee of any kind. I wrote it to get you thinking about retirement before it happens.

Too many times over the years, I've met with people who've already made the leap into retirement without any real direction or thought. They want a lifestyle that doesn't match up with their finances; they make decisions based on what may or may not be working for someone else.

As you read this book, I want you to create a retirement life that is yours. Your dreams, goals, and ambitions should be based on your situation. To do this, we'll create a vision, assess your situation, and prepare for the unexpected.

Read this book a few times—throw it in your briefcase, on your nightstand, in a desk drawer. Make sure it's somewhere accessible. This is an interactive book. Answer the questions at the end of each section, be honest, and share your answers with your spouse.

More important, read this book before you retire, so you can hit the ground running on the day you declare yourself retired.

Last, I want this book to get you thinking. You have to make these decisions once in your life, and there are pros and cons for each decision. Don't hesitate to seek out the advice of a financial professional for further input on creating a retirement plan that will fit your needs.

1

See Your Future

Dream a Little Dream

It's 5:45 in the morning and Tom and Mary are lost in their version of the same dream. It's one they've both been having for the past few months.

Tom's dream is that he is lying in the grass beside his grandson on a riverbank. They're watching the clouds float by and comparing thoughts about their shapes. They see boats, cows, and a car. Nearby, two fishing rods rest at an angle held up by two forked sticks pushed into the ground. Their tips are pointing toward the sky. Suddenly a rod tip bends and together they yell their battle cry: Fish on. They scramble to their feet.

In her version, Mary has just finished a pastry course at a prestigious culinary institute. Two days later she is contacted to fill in at an important political dinner at a four-star restaurant. Her specialty dessert is a success; she hears the room erupt in applause. Diners are calling her name and asking her to take a bow for her creation. The restaurant owner offers her the position of head pastry chef.

The sound of the alarm clock jolts Tom and Mary awake. They roll over, say their good mornings, and then follow a ritual that began about six months ago. Each reaches into the drawer of the nightstand on either side of the bed. They pull out identical day-to-day pocket calendars, cross out today's date, and flip forward to 147 days in the future—a day that's circled in red, a day they've thought about for the last twenty years. Now, as it gets closer, they feel the rush, shake a little, and sometimes giggle to themselves.

This is their retirement day, the day they've decided to walk away from their nine-to-five jobs and begin a new life. They stare at the page on their calendars for a few minutes trying to bring back their dreams, then sigh in unison. They close their calendars and get ready to get through another day. Another day that will bring them closer to the date circled in red.

WORKSHEET

One hundred and forty-seven days to go before Tom and Mary reach their day. They have been thinking about this for a long time.

When you dream about your retirement, what do you see?

When will it happen?

What will it be like not getting up and going to work following the same routines that you have followed for the past twenty years?

When Will It Come for You?

That day in red is coming for all of us. You might consider yourself retired because you're leaving the job you have been doing for the last ten or twenty years to start a new career. It might be the day you decide you're going to hang up your suit, put your dress shoes in the bottom of the closet, and wear only jeans and the old concert T-shirts from the 1960s and 1970s you've been saving. Perhaps it is the day you go back to school, start working part time, or volunteer for an organization. Maybe it's the day you purchase your tickets for that long trip to the Caribbean.

WORKSHEET

How will you define your retirement?

Why have you chosen to retire at this time?

How have you prepared for your retirement?

Then and Now

You might be fifty-five, sixty-five, or seventy years old when you decide you're ready to retire. However, have you thought about what retirement life will be like for you? Back in 1935, when Social Security began, retirement age and life expectancy were almost the same number. When you retired, you didn't buy green bananas because you couldn't be sure you'd be around to see them ripen. Retirement was a way to get an aging population out of the physically demanding jobs of the Industrial Age and replace them with younger and stronger muscles, not to create a lifestyle that would last twenty to thirty years (and longer for some). People gave little thought as to how they would spend their retirement back then; most were not expecting to be around to enjoy it.

Things are different now. Between 1946 and 1964, during the postwar baby boom, more than 78 million Americans made their appearance, and now sixty years later, the world is getting ready for us. Our retirement lifestyle will be much different from that of our parents.

In general, we'll live longer and be healthier. Average life expectancy is around eighty-six years. If you're sixty-five, there is about a 60 percent chance that you or your spouse will make it to age ninety and a 40 percent chance that one of you will make it to ninety-five. Some of us will be in retirement almost as long as we were in the workforce. That's twenty to thirty years in retirement longer than it was seventy-plus years ago.

It's going to be different, and the world is getting ready for you. Watch TV on any given night and you'll see advertising by most of the large financial companies talking about the retirement tsunami that's approaching. States and cities across the country are introducing legislation to address the needs of aging baby boomers. Companies are looking to hire people who have retired from their traditional careers but want to continue working in the form of consultants or part-time employees.

Travel, recreation, housing, health care, finance, and employment— they're all getting ready for you!

Staying Active

Boomers are concerned about their health, and are proactive about staying in shape. Visit the local school track on any spring or summer evening and you'll see groups of people, couples and individuals, walking and running to stay active and improve their health. Go to a large shopping mall early in the morning and you'll see people walking laps. The malls are encouraging it; many have even set up distance markers.

I read recently that even adventure activities like hiking, kayaking, and river rafting are generating participants among baby boomers.

Just because you're getting older doesn't mean you have to give up that competitive spirit. More and more boomers are involved in team sports like softball and doubles tennis or competitive swimming and running events.

Activity is one of the keys to a longer life, whether you choose to golf, bowl, dance, run, or walk. The physical and social benefits of taking part in an active lifestyle are key to living a long and fulfilling life. We have the opportunities, and most of us want to continue with our active lifestyles as long as our health allows.

Work a Passion Not a Job

Your desire to stay active will keep you physically fit and sharper mentally. Many of us will find that we still want to or, in some cases, have to continue to be productive. About 80 percent of the boomers retiring say they would like to continue to work. We may not want to continue in the same job, but this could be the opportunity to try something new. Think about what you enjoy and look for work in that field. For the hobby rose grower, for example, this could be the time to leave the desk and work at a garden center. If you're an amateur chef, you can now work in a restaurant.

It's not always easy to quit cold turkey. Think about why you want to go back to work and what you want or need to get from it. Is it a sense of accomplishment? Is it income to live on? Do you miss the friendships, or is it boredom? Take time to match the job you choose with the need it will fulfill.

I have a friend who worked as a sales manager for a tech company. He liked his job and was good at it, but after twenty years of stress and being away from home for long periods, he was ready to call it quits. I asked him what he was going to do.

"You know, I just can't stop working," he said, "but I'm going to do something I enjoy. This job won't be about the money—it will be about me."

His passion was fishing. Any free time he had, he would sneak away with his son or his friends and chase the latest lake legend.

I saw him a few months ago and asked how things were.

"I retired from ABC Co. with my retirement plan's stock options, and because my wife wants to continue to work for the next several years, we look pretty good financially," he told me. "So, I started working as the store manager for my buddy's bait-and-tackle shop and it's the best job I've had. I get there at five in the morning, dressed in T-shirt, shorts, and sandals. Then I start the coffee and get things ready for the early-morning guys.

"They usually get in around mid-morning and stop by to let me know what's biting and what's working. Then the afternoon guys come in around three and someone always talks me into going out with him for a couple of hours before dinner.

"You know, it seems as though I'm at the shop almost as many hours as I worked at ABC, but I'm there because I want to be there. I hang out with my friends and talk fishing all day. My wife and kids are happy because when I get home, I don't bring the stress of my job with me, and I always walk in the door smiling."

Take the time to match the job you choose with the need it will fulfill.

WORKSHEET

What are the activities you will enjoy during retirement?

Will you consider working during your retirement?

If you continue to work what will be the driving force behind it, (i.e., need income, want to remain productive, miss friendships)?

Will you continue with a former career or try something new?

Desire to Learn

A recent article mentioned that many retirees are relocating in towns that have colleges and universities. These people are looking for the opportunity to continue to learn and to interact with younger people in an academic environment to keep their minds sharp. We're born with a curiosity and desire to learn that can stay with us throughout our lives. Mary's dream was to return to school and become a pastry chef, a lifelong passion. She's definitely not ready to retire to the couch.

It's funny that to retire refers to going from an active state to one of inactivity. For most of us, retirement will mean going from one activity to another activity. So much more of the world has become available to us. Technology has opened doors and given us the ability to see and do things we only dreamed about growing up. We are the most computer-savvy group of retirees so far, and through the Internet we can work from home, e-mail a friend, book trips, research hobbies, take classes, or play Texas hold 'em poker with people on the other side of the world.

> Physical activity, mental challenges, time spent enjoying the company of family and friends: These are keys to longevity. Retirement shouldn't be a time to slow down and fade away; it should be a time to go full tilt, a time to use these keys to continue living the type of life we want to live.

It Won't Be All Roses

Retirement will have its challenges. Our longer life expectancy will create stress for those living on fixed incomes. The effects of inflation over time and not enough savings for a twenty-year or thirty-year retirement are cause for concern. The possibility of outliving our income and cash resources hangs over many of us.

The disappearance of the traditional pension plan and the concerns of Social Security have taken away what have been in the past a security blanket to support the retiree. Each year, close to a thousand employers close their defined benefit plans. It has become our responsibility to save for our own retirement, and most people are lagging. More than half of Americans saving for retirement have less than $50,000 set aside.

For those of us living on a fixed income, inflation will erode purchasing power each year. To maintain the same standard of living year after year, you have to be able to increase your income at least to the level of inflation. If not, the same amount of money will buy fewer goods. For someone in retirement for twenty-five years, costs can easily double. If you want some examples, consider the postage stamp, gasoline, and food prices.

Rising health care costs, concerns about Medicare, and increasing prescription prices as well as the possible need for long-term care can quickly eat up a lifetime of savings. Medical expenses for a couple of sixty-five-year-olds can run as high as $300,000, inflation adjusted to cover Medicare premiums. Moreover, a longer life expectancy increases the potential for long-term care needs, which can run as high as $70,000 a year in today's dollars.

Another concern is that retirement is a long time, and that we probably will not increase our savings substantially even if we continue to work. Overspending of our retirement savings in the early years and poor money management can have a lasting effect on our account values that may be impossible to recoup.

2

CREATE A PLAN

Lay the Groundwork

Retirement is a transition, just like when we went from being a child to adulthood. As adults, we took on the responsibility of how we would shape our life. Perhaps when we were getting engaged to be married, we and our future husband or wife talked about where we would like to live, how many children we would have, what or where our first home would be, and how we would manage finances. As time went on, we discussed our children's education, and how to save for it. We started looking to the future, paying for weddings, funding our retirement, and enjoying grandchildren.

All of our plans may not have worked out exactly as we originally envisioned them—adjustments were made, plans changed—but we had a basic plan that guided us. We talked and pictured the life we wanted to live, and made adjustments as new situations presented themselves.

Now we are entering a new phase of life, and this new phase will need a new plan. Perhaps you have thoughts about what it will be like, what you'll do, and when it will happen.

Up to this point, most of us have prepared for retirement by saving in our 401(k) and any of the other employer-sponsored plans as well as our IRAs. We had a savings goal number we had read about in a magazine or we went to a Web site and used its retirement planner to tell us what we needed. When we got our quarterly statements, we looked at the total number and benchmarked it against a number we had read about, or perhaps we compared our totals with those of our friends. Depending on how they matched up to our benchmarks, we felt either accomplished and confident that we would have the retirement of our dreams or depressed that we would never win the rat race.

The problem with these numbers is that they never look at our unique situations. They don't know our goals or dreams; they don't know what's important to us about our money.

That's why it's crucial for us to take time to create a plan for our retirement. Think about what's important for you in your retirement. Create a vision of what your retirement will be like. Write down your dreams, your goals, and the lifestyle you would like. Then think about how you'll accomplish them. Create a cash-flow statement, understand your costs, and know where your income will be coming from. Make sure your basic needs are covered. Consider how you will fund your dreams and goals, and set priorities. Break your overall retirement dream into smaller sections; five years is a good period. Use the five-year time horizon to set up your budget, looking at cash flow in, and out. Decide which of your dreams and goals you want to accomplish during these five years. You probably have a million things you want to do. It's not necessary to do them all in the first six months of retirement. Plan them out, and time them to match your current finances. You may need to make adjustments to meet these goals in your lifestyle.

What's more important, paying the mortgage or dinner out three nights a week? Should you think about working part time to pay for an annual vacation rather than deplete retirement savings?

In addition, through this retirement time we need to make sure that we've prepared for the unexpected. Make sure there is a plan B in case something happens to you, your spouse or your partner.

CHECKLIST

❑ Create your vision of your retirement.

❑ Plan a strategy.

❑ Prepare for the unexpected.

Are You Ready?

For some of us, retirement life will be just like on the commercials we see. We prepared well, saved a bundle, made the right investments at the right time, and earned enough money during our working years to allow us to do that. Retirement will be a new vacation home, an annual trip to Europe, perhaps a world cruise. Others of us who have prepared equally well may want to remain productive, or still need the feeling of accomplishment. We may want to go back to school, volunteer to work with a charitable group, or even sit down and write the Great American Novel. For those of you who enter retirement in this situation, I applaud and admire you. You've done it! For you, retirement will be exactly what you expected.

A lot of us might be more concerned about what will happen to us at our retirement. For us, part of planning will be in survival mode. Am I able to do this? Can I really make this change? The inability for us to prepare for the retirement we want during our working years may force us to delay retirement, not because we aren't ready to retire but because we need to survive. Weak economies, bad stock markets, education costs for children, and health issues—these are just a few factors that could affect our ability to be as prepared for retirement as we had hoped. If you're entering retirement playing catch-up, you'll require even tighter controls and monitoring.

WORKSHEET

What are some of your concerns when you think of entering retirement. Are they financial, health, or perhaps you worry that you'll be bored?

Have you prepared well or will day-to-day living be a concern?

Think It, Write It, Share It

Now let's sketch out a plan, not a set-in-stone plan but rather some thoughts and ideas. Get a small pocket notebook/calendar, one for you and one for the person with whom you're going to spend your retirement years. Get something that's small enough to carry in your pocket or briefcase. Circle the day in the calendar you want to retire, it doesn't have to be exact but pick a time you think will be close. Show this date to the person with whom you will spend retirement; let your partner know why you feel this date is the right one. Listen to his or her questions about why you chose this date. Share and listen. Circle your spouse's retirement date on your calendar also.

Answer the questions from the worksheets provided throughout the book. These questions are meant to start you thinking about your retirement. As you work through the questions provided I hope you begin to raise questions of your own. The questions you bring up are what will make your retirement plan unique to you. These questions will pertain to your individual situation, your concerns, and your thoughts and values.

It is important that both you and your spouse keep your own notebooks and calendars. You should write your thoughts before you sit down and share them. Sharing thoughts can be an awkward experience even for couples who have been together for years. It's one thing to share candy, cookies, or the blankets on a cold winter night, but we don't always share thoughts with those we know best. I wonder if this is because we become so familiar with someone that we make assumptions. We tend to assume that our spouse or companion has the same thoughts about the next twenty years as we do.

But this is different. This is a life change and each of you in the back of your mind has had growing an idea about what your life together will be like during retirement. It's time to break away from the routine that has ruled your daily life for the last twenty-plus years. Because these are dreams of the future, have you ever really talked about them? Will they remain just dreams because you just continued to play follow the leader without ever realizing your spouse had dreams of his or her own? Can you imagine the problem that would arise with a couple retiring on the same day who never really discussed, just assumed? Scenario: A husband shows up at home towing a brand-new $50,000 bass boat with his and hers swivel seats, pulls into the driveway, and says, "You have to come out and see what I bought for our retirement."

His wife says, "Okay, but before we go I just wanted to let you know that I have been accepted to a three-year internship at an art colony in the Arizona desert. Isn't that great?"

WORKSHEET

Visualize your retirement, write down your ideas and share them with your partner. This is a big step to ensure that you both know what the other wants.

Remember when you first started building your family? You were young and had big dreams about where you would live, how many children you would have, where they would go to college, their weddings, and your grandchildren. How many nights did you sit and share with your partner what you thought life would be like?

The Big Picture

Next, put your feet up, your head back, and picture the retirement you want. What are the big dreams? What are the things you've always wanted to do? Is it to travel to Europe? Would you like to go back to school, perhaps buy a vacation home? Some dreams may not happen until after you're gone; maybe you wanted to make sure your grandchild's college education was paid, but weren't sure you would be around to see her graduate. At least you'll have the satisfaction of knowing you'll be taking part in the future event.

Now that you've thought about the big dreams, sit down with your spouse or companion and (that's right) share your thoughts. Talk about your ideas, talk about the things you want to do, and listen. This is your retirement together. Listen to your mate, give him or her the chance to share dreams and visions. Talk about what your life will be like when you leave your traditional jobs and begin your new life.

Write your thoughts on the left-hand page of your notebook and have your partner write their thoughts on the right, and you do the same in theirs. This will allow you to see these thoughts together.

> Keep your notebook close and look at it often.

Leave the Driver in the Bag

Now that you and your spouse know each other's big picture of retirement and what you want to do, it is time to think about when you want to do them. Chances are your intentions are not to do everything in the first year or two; it is not practical. It would be similar to going to Disneyland for a month and riding all the rides in the first hour. So, take your big-picture goals and break them down into segments, looking at five-year periods.

First, you need to prioritize them. Which goal is the most important to complete at this time? There may be financial reasons for making a goal a priority; it may be more or less expensive at a certain time or you may have funds more readily available at one time or another. It may make more sense to set a high priority on more physically demanding events earlier in retirement than later. Climbing Mount Everest might be easier at sixty-five than eighty-five.

Within the group of friends with whom I hang out, I'm without a doubt the worst golfer. Before I even get to the tee box to look at the hole, I have my driver out and a grip-it-and-rip-it attitude. On every par 4 or 5 I use my driver off the tee with no consideration of what the hole looks like. This usually puts me in the next fairway, or the woods, or in a hazard!

It's usually a drop with a penalty or a couple of shots to get back into play, then I just go for the green because I've hit so many bad shots. I'm sure I have a miracle shot in me that will put me within a couple of inches of the cup for a tap-in to save the hole. It never works. I usually get frustrated, my vocabulary becomes very colorful, and my friends are already thinking about the lunch and beers I'll have to buy at the turn.

One day after a typical start—two double bogeys, one triple bogey, and two lost balls—we walked up to the fourth hole, a tight 510-yard par 5 with a brook running across the fairway about 75 yards from the hole. I was still steaming from the last hole and reached for my driver: I was going to cream it.

All of a sudden, my partner said, "Stop before you pick a club. Walk up to the tee box and look at the hole." He walked over with me and said, "How are you going to play this?"

"Driver down the middle, five iron over the brook, chip on, and two-putt."

"That's how to go at it, Mike," our opponents yelled. They were looking at the lunch menu, figuring I'd get a big number on the hole and I'd be buying them an even bigger lunch.

My partner said, "Look at the hole and think of a plan. You aren't Tiger Woods and you haven't hit your driver decently all day. Hit a five iron off the tee. You hit that club consistently straight and about 190 yards. Next, hit your seven-iron and lay up before the brook; if you try to go over, you'll swing too hard and hit a bad shot, or if you get lucky and hit a good shot, you'll probably end up wet! Leave yourself about 125 yards to the hole, a nice pitch for you. It's a par five, so break down the hole into five reasonable shots. Three controlled 170-yard shots will get you there a lot easier than trying to hit a wild 250-yard drive that will probably end up unplayable and leave you scrambling just to get back into play."

Well, I followed his plan and didn't par the hole; I missed my putt. But for the rest of the day, before I took a club out of my bag I looked over the hole, went to the tee box empty-handed, and took an overview. I then envisioned three manageable, controlled shots I knew I could hit.

The rest of the afternoon was different from our usual game. I didn't lose any more balls; I didn't have a real reason to rant. I parred some holes and got a few bogeys but no big numbers—and I did not buy lunch.

Exercise: Physical and Mental

What will your first five years look like? How will you spend your weeks? How will you divide your time? Are you going to continue to work? Will it be twenty hours or forty hours? Maybe it will be seasonal or perhaps you'll create a situation in which you can choose your own hours.

What will your ideal week look like? How much time will you put in to stay in shape? Will your exercise regimen include an evening walk with friends, a regular tee time, or three visits a week to the gym? Perhaps you want to acquire a new skill, learn to dance, study karate, or get a couple of bicycles. Don't think you're too old or it's been too long since you last exercised. Studies have shown that even people in their eighties can benefit from exercise. Activity will add years to your life, it will keep you mentally sharper, it will give you more energy. Exercise can help to control certain medical conditions, keep you flexible, and keep your sex life hot. If you already exercise, good for you, keep it going. If exercise is one of your retirement goals, make sure you check with your doctor to see if you should be aware of any limitations.

How much time do you want to set aside for mental development? Your brain is just like any muscle in your body; it needs exercise on a regular basis. Is this the time to learn a language or finish the degree you started years ago? Maybe learn a musical instrument, or improve your computer skills?

You're Never Too Old

I recently read about a newly retired mother who was telling her son that she was thinking about going back to school to get the law degree she always wanted. Her son was surprised that at this point in her life she would take on such a big task, and at her age (she was sixty-two years old). She would not finish for three years, at which time she would be sixty-five. Her reasoning was that whether or not she went back to school she would still be sixty-five in three years' time. She felt her options were to be a sixty-five-year-old with a fulfilled dream or with an unfulfilled dream.

What a great story!

Take the Time to Reconnect

Now think about spending time with the people who are important to you. How much time do you want to spend strengthening or reestablishing relationships? Is there someone you feel you've neglected over the years, someone you take for granted because they were always around for you and it was a given that if you needed them, they would be there for you? This could be a spouse, a child, or a close friend. Is it time to reconnect, maybe time to close the distance, to give back some of that time?

As you look at your dreams and goals, think about them on the physical and emotional levels. After all those years of work and your busy day-to-day life, you start to lose your connection to people; you may take your relationships for granted. Do you sometimes feel that the only conversation at your house is "What's for dinner?" or "Where's the remote?" Friends you have been promising to ring up never receive that call. Time promised to children and grandchildren turns out to be so much shorter than you'd hoped. As you think about the weeks and months ahead, consider the time you want to spend rebuilding those connections. Fit it into your week. When I meet and talk with people about their retirement goals, spending time with their families is always a priority.

WORKSHEET

How will you spend your time?

What are the factors that will drive your activities?

List your big goals in order of importance and your reasons for assigning them their ranking.

WORKSHEET (continued)

Draw a timeline and put them along the line when you expect to accomplish them.

One More Time

Think about your big dreams. A few of us will be able to do all of them, when we want. The majority of us will have to plan when we can do them, and set priorities. Which are the most important for you? Once you have reviewed your financial situation, cash flow, and assets during retirement, you'll develop some direction as to when, how, and if you can make these big dreams happen.

Open your notebook and look at the words. Did you get everything? Don't worry if you didn't, as this is an ongoing process, I hope this part of retirement goes on forever. The part I'm talking about is the dreams, the desire to want to do more. This drive, this desire, is what will keep you going; it will add years to your life; it will drive you to live longer because you won't be ready to give up until you've done it all.

Break down your retirement years to shorter segments. Look at five-year periods for what you will want for your lifestyle. Which of the big dreams will fit into those five-year slots and when?

Write it down, and share what you've written with your spouse or companion. You've shared the growing years together, now you need to share this huge life-changing event. You need to visualize the next twenty-five or thirty years. Retirement is not something that sneaks up on you; your parents retired, your aunts and uncles retired, and through your working life you've been thinking about the day you'll retire. You save for your retirement at work through a 401(k). You contribute to Roth and traditional IRAs. You know friends who have retired or are close to retirement. The newspaper is loaded with articles on retirement; there are dozens of financial magazines with strategies to finance your retirement.

The movement of the postwar baby boomers into retirement is a phenomenon that is grabbing everyone's attention. Everyone, from financial planners, to travel agents, to health care practitioners, is getting ready for this time. Each has thoughts and ideas on what you need and how you should spend your retirement.

There's only one problem—they're not you! They're not your spouse; they don't know what your thoughts, or goals, or dreams are; they don't know about your finances; they don't know how much money you have or what your intentions for it are. They have some great thoughts, some great products, and some great ideas, but which ones are for you?

It's up to us to create our own retirement based on what we want to do, not on what someone else is doing or suggesting for his retirement. Our idea of retirement is unique to us. It's up to us to decide whether we'll continue to work or play. This is a decision based on our visions, visions of the retirement we are looking at now—before it happens. We are planning when it will happen based on a date we've sat down and discussed. It will be at a time that is to our advantage; we've sketched out the next several years in short, doable segments; we've talked about whether or not we'll continue to work; we have an idea of what we'd like our lifestyle to be, which of the dreams we want to fulfill and where they fit in.

This is your retirement. It's another leg of the relay race, childhood, adulthood, now retirement, and the finish line still is not in sight. Like a good athlete, you've done a lot of the prep work, so now it's time to envision the race you're going to run. It's good to know how to pace yourself, when to be ready for the hill climbs that can drain you and when to coast on the downhills and the flats.

3

Take Inventory

Time to Look at Money

Now you're starting to think about retirement. The vision of how you want to live it is coming into view and you're thinking that the next step is to jump in, right? Order those cruise tickets, buy that new car, book a month's worth of tee times.

Whoa, slow down for a second and catch your breath. You've painted a picture of what you would like your retirement to be, and like most people, chances are you painted your picture in a perfect world. The sun is always shining, you always catch your limit on that fishing boat. The twenty-five foot putts always go in, and you never step on your dance partner's toes. These are dreams—the perfect times.

The reality is that most of us won't live the perfect retirement dream. There'll be bumps and snags, along with the occasional nightmare. If you're reading this book, you've already experienced fifty-plus years of life and know what happens to the best laid plans.

We can't prepare for all the unexpected events we'll come across over the next twenty-five, thirty-five or, for some of us, the next forty years, but there is one area that will have the greatest influence on how you spend your retirement and that is: money, income, cash flow, savings, moolah, dinero, greenbacks, whatever you want to call it.

Money will decide when and if you can travel, whether you can afford to eat out three nights a week or once every couple of months. Money will influence your lifestyle and determine if you need to work. Money will have an impact on where you live—does it make sense to stay where you are or should you think about downsizing?

Money will determine the type of health care you can afford ,and insurance coverage. Money will determine how your spouse will live if you die first and how he or she will continue the retirement the two of you had dreamed of.

In order to do the kind of planning that will allow you to fulfill your dreams, you have to take a realistic look at the money situation. You need to have a solid idea of how things will change when you leave your current job, you need to know what your priorities are for spending, and you need to know where your shortfalls are and what you can do to overcome them.

One of the first things you must know is how much money you'll need in retirement. Most people have an inflated view of how much money they've saved and little understanding of how much money will be necessary to live on.

It's easy look at your retirement savings statement, see a five-digit or six-digit number, and believe you're fat with cash. After all, in many cases our retirement fund is without a doubt the largest amount of money we've ever been able to save.

The problem is that once we reach retirement age, we've probably saved as much money as we're going to save. Some of us may continue to work in retirement and continue to save for later years; however, most of us will keep our jobs to delay accessing our savings account or to make ends meet. The only growth to our savings will be in the form of interest or portfolio performance.

Now take a look at what you've saved toward retirement. Consider the fact that you will be in retirement for twenty-five or thirty years. Take the paycheck that you get every week out of the equation and replace it with the reduced income from Social Security, or if you're one of the lucky ones, maybe you will receive a pension. How does it look? Do you still feel flush? Does your retirement savings account look as big as it did a few moments ago?

> According to EBRI, 58 percent of Americans have not calculated how much money they will need at retirement.

> Thirty-eight percent of households headed by a person over eighty-five had less than $25,000 in non-housing assets.

Cash Flow

I asked you earlier to buy a notebook and write down your retirement dreams, because it's easier to visualize when you see the written word. As we talk about money, it becomes even more important to put it in writing. When you've written down the numbers and you can see the cash flow, it can be a revelation.

To get an idea of what you need, create a cash flow statement: simply put, cash flow in minus cash flow out. This will determine whether you have an excess or a deficit. First, you want to work with your basic living expenses—what we need to live on. Only after you've satisfied these basic needs can you consider your lifestyle expenses—how you live your life.

Where will the money come from? Start with income sources: Social Security, pensions, and continued employment. Then consider assets, 401(k), savings, IRAs and possible future money from an inheritance or the sale of a home. Many income options and retirement savings accounts have their own peculiarities and consequences for withdrawals. It is important to understand how these accounts work before you take money out.

This is not meant to be a strategy session; I can recommend a strategy to you only after an in-depth discussion and analysis of your individual situation. However, some general knowledge and information will help prepare you and give some direction as you get closer to retirement.

Remember, this is not a solo act. Sit down with your spouse or partner and plan together. You both have created this dream, worked for this time, and now it's most important that you continue to work together to make it happen.

Do You Really Know What You Need?

First, you must determine what it costs you to live each month. This will be the essential bills, housing, food, heat, insurance, taxes, medical, and transportation. I want to make sure that you have these covered before anything else. You need these bills paid for survival, and there is rarely any wiggle room. It's also important to pay attention to the dates any of these payments will end, like a mortgage or a car payment.

Next, create a list of all possible income, savings, and future cash sources (inheritance, sale of property). These should be solid sources—don't include the possibility of winning your state lottery; it's not reliable enough.

Once you've put these numbers together, it's important to have a cash reserve set aside to cover emergencies. These could be household, personal, or health issues, unexpected in nature, and if not prepared for, they could disrupt your income needs.

Now consider your lifestyle costs and needs. This is your fun money, the money that pays for recreation, Saturday-night dinner and a movie, trips to visit the grandchildren, or vacations.

Last, think about money for other purposes. This is the money you want to leave to your children to give them a kick-start at their own family life, to pay for a grandchild's education, money you want to leave to a charity. This money becomes your legacy: This is how your family will continue your retirement dreams and fulfill them when you're gone.

The main issues I see when doing planning for people, especially those who have retired or are close to retirement, are how much money they need to live on and how far into retirement their money will take them.

What I find is that while people are working and receiving a weekly paycheck, they feel secure. They have an inflated view about the money they've accumulated. They think because their parents lived on a hundred dollars a week in retirement, they can too. They forget about the fact that their retirement is going to last twenty-five or thirty years. They don't realize that drawing large amounts of money in the early years of retirement can have adverse effects later on. They don't realize the effect higher prices or inflation will have ten or twenty years from now. What they really need to consider is: What will life be like when that paycheck stops?

Bills will not stop when the paycheck stops; you won't need less food; you won't need less heat for the house; and the mortgage ends in thirty years whether you are getting a paycheck or not. You must be ready when that regular paycheck ends— you have to start preparing now.

Social Security will replace part of your income. If you're lucky, you'll get a pension from work to replace part of your income; the rest will come from savings and continued employment.

> Prepare yourself now. Know what you'll be up against and be ready.

Necessary Monthly Expenses

So let's look at what it costs you to live each month. Grab your checkbook or open up your computer and start making a list of costs. Use the worksheet starting on page 34 to guide you along, and don't cheat. Consider everything you need to exist. If not paying a bill will affect basic living needs or land you in jail, it should be on the list. If it's not a monthly or weekly cost, like house taxes, take the number and divide by twelve, so you can spread it out over twelve months. Make sure you get everything: food, housing, fuel, car payments, taxes, insurance, utilities. These are your monthly costs; what you need to survive. Follow the worksheet—it will help to make it easier.

When you look at costs that fluctuate, get an average cost. If your heating costs are $200 one month and $500 another, calculate the average annual cost and use that.

For debt payments like credit cards, look at the balances and charging patterns. Do you pay off your card each month or are you carrying a balance and making payments to whittle it down?

For mortgages and car loans, know the monthly payment, lump sum, rate, and end date of payment.

What you're looking to establish here is a pattern of monthly necessary cash outflows. At this time, don't include what I'm going to refer to as lifestyle expenses. These expenses are those that aren't necessary to live on, even though you may have included them in your monthly budget while you were still working. Lifestyle expenses may include travel, recreation, lunch with friends, tee times, a day at the spa. These are all things you enjoy and that had become part of your lifestyle in your working years, when that paycheck was coming in.

Now that your regularly scheduled, dependable, like-clockwork paycheck is gone, you may have to live on a reduced income, and that reduced income will determine priorities in your spending patterns. The first priorities are food and shelter; you have to eat, and food and housing must be taken care of before you can play. How much fun would a round of golf be if you had to skip meals and a mortgage payment just to afford to play?

MONTHLY EXPENSE WORKSHEET

Basic Life Expenses	Monthly	Annually
HOUSING		
Mortgage/Rent		
Taxes		
Insurance		
Utilities		
Electricity/Gas		
Telephone		
Water/Sewer		
FOOD		
CLOTHING		
TRANSPORTATION		
Car Payment		
Auto Insurance		
Fuel		
Maintenance		
HEALTHCARE		
Insurance		
Medications		
Out-of-pocket		
Life Insurance		
Long-term Care		
PERSONAL DEBT		
MISCELLANEOUS		

WORKSHEET

Now that you've listed your basic monthly expenses, take a long, hard look at them. Are there any surprises? Were you close in your estimate or are you substantially higher or lower?

Concerning credit cards: Are you paying just the minimum each month and dragging the payment out so it becomes a regular monthly cost?

Solutions:

What about your mortgage payment and your car payments? Are you on schedule to pay those off as you had planned?

Solutions:

WORKSHEET (continued)

Over the next few years, do you see your monthly living costs increasing or decreasing? By how much?

Solutions:

In which area do you see your costs changing and what would be the reasons for the changes?

Solutions:

How will rising prices affect your ability to maintain your basic life expenses?

Solutions:

Plan B

With the worksheet in the last section complete, you have a good idea of what you need to survive each month. You know what your living expenses are and can plan your income to pay these bills.

How have you prepared for the unexpected events that always seem to appear? What about the emergency that shows up without warning? Your car breaks down; your house needs an immediate repair; you incur an uncovered medical expense. You may have to cover an expense for a short time until you receive reimbursement from a third party. These are all situations—and there are many more—that require an immediate payment from you to correct the problem. So where will the money come from to cover the unexpected?

Money set aside for emergencies needs to be liquid. Money market accounts, savings accounts, even short-term CDs (some may allow liquidity, or minimal charges to break the term) are the types of accounts that work best.

This money should not be part of the retirement plan you have with your employer. Getting money from this kind of plan takes time, creates taxes, and often has restrictions to certain types of withdrawals. Some plans allow for loans, but only if you're employed by the employer sponsoring the plan. However, once you've retired or left the company, you can't borrow against the plan. Also, any unpaid balances will be treated as a distribution to you; taxed and if you are under 59½ may be subject to an additional 10 percent penalty.

IRAs can hold cash positions like savings accounts, money markets, and CDs, but remember, withdrawals will be taxable to you. If you have a substantial emergency expense, you'll owe taxes at your tax rate for the withdrawal. This can really be a problem if on April 15 of the following year you don't have the money to pay the taxes; you have to make another withdrawal, which creates another taxable withdrawal for the following year. I'm assuming if you are reading this that you are or will be at least 59½ years old. If you are younger and need to take money from your IRA, you will also have a 10 percent early-withdrawal penalty on the amount.

Nonretirement accounts are the preferred source of emergency funds, but even among these, some options are better than others. It is important to understand any restrictions, penalties, or charges that may apply. Usually if a product guarantees a rate of return for a certain period, there is a consequence for early withdrawal.

Investment portfolios, stocks, bonds, and mutual funds can be sold to generate cash if necessary, but they're a poor choice for emergency money. The downside here is transaction costs, possible capital gains tax, and selling at an inopportune time. It may be necessary to sell during a market downswing, at a loss.

Even though cash accounts like money markets and savings will probably offer the lowest rates of return, their liquidity features and lack of tax consequences make them the right place to park your emergency funds.

How much you should keep in this emergency account is something you will have to decide. If your income was disrupted for a period of time, how would you pay your bills? Look at your insurance policies; make sure there is enough to cover deductibles and out-of-pocket costs. Survey your house. Are there any areas of concern? What about your vehicles? Are they reliable and trouble-free or do they have 200,000 miles and have trouble making it out of the driveway?

Once you have set up an emergency fund, make a commitment not to touch it for anything other than emergencies. This should not be an account you use for vacation or borrow from for other expenses. It's easy to take money from this account with the intention of paying it back later. However, emergencies are not everyday events; sometimes they don't happen for years. The longer you go without a problem, the longer you'll delay paying back your emergency fund. Then when the day comes that you need it, you'll have to access one of the less favorable accounts.

CHECKLIST

❑ Review your situation and set aside an amount in your emergency account, with which you are comfortable, in order to cover any unforeseen events.

❑ Make sure it is liquid and available.

❑ Make the commitment to yourself that this account is for emergencies only, and if you need to withdraw from this account, make it a priority to replenish the account ASAP.

Income and Savings

Okay, by now you should have an idea of your current necessary expenses and have determined the amount you're comfortable with for emergencies. Remember, these first numbers are basic expense numbers only. You shouldn't have any lifestyle expenses built into your calculations yet. We're coming to spending the fun money soon, but first you need to see how your income and savings stack up against your bills.

So, how are you going to cover your bills? Will you be receiving income during your retirement, from Social Security, a pension, or continued employment? Perhaps you will cover your expenses by withdrawing from your retirement savings accounts, your 401(k)s and IRAs.

As you start to plan your retirement income, it's important to understand your options, and the rules that go along with them.

Social Security, which will be a source of income for nearly all retirees, requires planning before you start to receive it. The age you start Social Security will affect the amount of your benefit. If you're still working when you begin benefits, it may or may not affect the amount you receive.

If you have a pension plan, you must decide whether you want to receive a lifetime income, or you may have the option to do a direct rollover to an IRA. If you choose to take an income, should you take a larger payout based on your single life expectancy or would a reduced payout based on a joint life expectancy that will provide income through your surviving spouse's lifetime be better?

How will you use the money you've accumulated in retirement savings plans and IRAs? Will you convert these to an income stream, take irregular distributions, or delay using them to a later date? Do you understand how they will affect your taxes? Do you know when you must begin withdrawals? How much are you required to withdraw? What are the problems that can arise if you don't begin distributions at the required time?

So, before you make a snap decision on how you'll generate your income, let's take a few minutes to understand the basics of your income sources and how to use the rules and options to your advantage.

Social Security

When most people think of retirement income, Social Security is usually the first source that comes to mind. The federal government guarantees you payments for life along with an annual cost-of-living adjustment.

> For more than 20 percent of the retirees over age sixty-five, Social Security is their only source of income, and for more than 65 percent, it is at least half.

During our working life, we and our employers have been contributing to our Social Security benefit through FICA withholding. Each pay period, 15.3 percent of our income goes toward our Social Security and Medicare benefits. We contribute 7.65 percent and our employer contributes 7.65 percent on our behalf. If you're self-employed, you pay the full amount. Out of the 7.65 percent withheld, 6.2 percent goes for Social Security benefits and the 1.45 percent remaining goes for Medicare benefits.

To qualify for full Social Security benefits, you must have an earnings history for at least forty quarters (ten years).

Benefits can be paid in three possible ways:

1) to you, based on your earnings;
2) as a reduced amount to a spouse, based on a working spouse's benefit;
   or
3) as a survivor benefit equal to the deceased spouse's benefit if it exceeds your own.

If both spouses are receiving their own benefits based on their individual earnings, Social Security will not continue to pay theirs and the survivor benefit, only the larger.

Some of your Social security may be taxable too. If your adjusted gross income plus non-taxable income plus 50 percent of your Social Security benefit is above a certain threshold, you may have to pay taxes on a portion of your benefit. A married couple with this combined income between $32,000 and $44,000 may pay taxes on 50 percent of their benefit. A couple with over $44,000 may pay taxes on 85 percent of their benefit.

You can start getting benefits as early as age sixty-two at a reduced amount or wait until full retirement age to receive full benefits. The year you were born decides your full retirement age. If you were born before 1938, your full retirement age is sixty-five. This gradually increases to age sixty-seven for those born in 1960 and later.

Planning for Your Benefits

The biggest planning issue most people have regarding their Social Security benefit is: When should I start? Before you rush down to sign up to receive your first check, you'll want to understand some of the options and their effects.

At age sixty-two, you'll become eligible for a reduced benefit of the amount payable to you at full retirement age. The reduction is around 25 percent for those born before 1954 and 30 percent for those born after 1954. This reduced benefit will be paid to you and continue to your surviving spouse if applicable. The common thought by most is that the sooner you start to receive your benefits, the more money you'll collect during your lifetime.

If you're thinking along these lines, stop and calculate your break-even age. People with a full retirement age of sixty-six years taking a reduced benefit at sixty-two versus taking a full benefit at age sixty-six break even at around age seventy-eight. With today's longer life expectancies, most of us will live many years longer than the break-even mark. Remember, your surviving spouse will receive your benefit if it's higher than his or hers. When you start receiving your benefit may directly affect how much money he or she will receive if you die first.

Another issue that will affect your benefit if you're considering taking a payout before full retirement age is employment. If you continue to work, earn W2 wages, and collect benefits before full retirement age, you may see a reduction in benefits. If you are under full retirement age and collect benefits, your payment is reduced one dollar for every two dollars you earn above the annual limit. In 2007, the limit was $12,960. In the year you reach full retirement age, your benefit reduction is one dollar for every three dollars earned and your annual earnings limit will increase to $34,440 (in 2007). Starting the month you reach full retirement age, there are no limits or reductions concerning earnings and benefits.

Waiting until full retirement age before starting benefits means you can work and earn as much as you want without a reduction in payments. Your surviving spouse will receive a benefit equal to 100 percent of your benefit or his or her own benefit, whichever is higher.

Those of you who want to delay benefits past full retirement age can see an increase in benefit of up to 8 percent per year that you delay, up to age seventy. It might make sense for someone still working to delay taking benefits for a larger amount later, when there is no longer a need or desire to work, or to provide a larger survivor's benefit.

If you think you may miss out by waiting to take a delayed benefit, the break-even mark is around eighty-three years old. Delaying your benefit until age seventy can be a sound strategy if you're trying to maximize your survivor benefit. This could be especially important if you have pension or annuity payouts that end at your death or if your spouse is several years younger.

WORKSHEET

When will you start your benefits?

Will continued employment be a factor?

Can you afford to wait for a higher benefit?

How will your benefit provide for your spouse if he or she survives you?

EXAMPLE

Assumptions: January 1, 2007
Full retirement age 65 years 8 months

Age 62	**Age 65** (reaches FRA in Nov. 2007)
$ 1,000/month Social Security	$ 1,000/month Social Security
$22,000 annual earnings from work	$45,000 annual earnings from work
[Reduction in benefit]	[Reduction in benefit]
($12,960) (annual earnings limit)	($34,440) (annual earnings limit)
$9,040 ÷ 2 = $4,520 reduction in benefits	$10,560 ÷ 3 = $3,520 reduction in benefits

The Pension Disappearing Act

Over the past five to ten years, one of the foundations of most people's retirement plan, the defined benefit retirement pension, has been disappearing. The way these plans worked was an employer would provide a retirement benefit usually based on a formula that combined earnings and years of service. In order to do that, he had to assume the contributions and investment risk. It was the obligation of the company to make sure that money was available to you at your retirement.

The employer had to make periodic contributions to make sure the plan had adequate funds to provide an annuity payout equal to the defined amount at retirement. The amounts needed and earnings were actuarially determined. The actuary had to constantly review the plan to make sure it was on track. If the investment performance was less than expected, the employer was required to make up the difference. Plans could even become overfunded in which case contributions were halted for a period.

Defined benefit pensions provided security and confidence during retirement by presenting us with a regular, dependable income. Along with a Social Security benefit, these plans provided the recipient with an income for life and survivorship benefits.

Because these plans are expensive to administer and the employer is responsible for investment performance, these plans have begun to disappear. They have been replaced with defined contribution plans [401(k)]. These plans are almost the opposite of the pension plan. In the defined contribution plan, the only known number is the contribution. You, the employee, assume the investment risk by making your own investment choices, usually from a menu of mutual fund–type products. The obligation of providing you with a retirement benefit transfers from the employer to you, the employee.

Some of you may be lucky enough to work for companies that still have a defined benefit pension plan. If you do, pay close attention to the payout options. A single life expectancy payout will provide you with the most money each month but the payouts may end at your death—that is, with no benefit for your surviving spouse. Survivorship options usually are 50 percent to you during your lifetime and 50 percent to your surviving spouse, or 66⅔ percent to you and 33⅓ percent to the survivor.

It's important to review all income options. Remember, not only do you need to think about income during your lifetime, but you also have to think about providing for the surviving spouse. If both you and your spouse will receive adequate lifetime income from your individual sources, both of you may decide that the larger single life option is best. Income from your plan will end at your death, and your spouse will continue to support him- or herself with his own income source. If the surviving spouse doesn't have adequate income sources of his or her own, it may be necessary to take a lesser amount now and guarantee a survivor benefit.

Another option is to delay your Social Security until you reach a higher benefit level. This might allow you to take a higher lifetime benefit now and give your beneficiary a higher Social Security benefit at your death. A common tactic is to purchase a life insurance policy, to guarantee your spouse enough money to live on after your death. This will allow you to take the single life benefit and receive the larger payout. Meanwhile, purchase a life insurance policy with a death benefit high enough to provide your spouse with enough money to live on. At your death, when he or she receives the benefit, she can invest it and use it when necessary or create her own income stream.

You must consider and plan for your income needs before retirement. The choices you make concerning your payout are irrevocable. If you choose a single life payout and in a couple of years something happens to you, your spouse cannot go back and say, "Whoops, we made the wrong decision." If using the strategy of purchasing life insurance, you need to know if you are insurable at a reasonable rate and how much income you will want to replace, and have the policy issued before you choose your payout option.

> Knowing and understanding your income sources will help to make some of your most important pre-retirement choices.

Checklist

❑ If you don't know your Social Security benefit payouts at different ages, contact your local Social Security office.

❑ Contact your HR department to learn about the options available to you regarding your defined benefit pension.

❑ Make sure you sit down and discuss your options with your spouse, and don't hesitate to bring in a financial planner to review various scenarios.

Comparing Ins and Outs

By now you should have an idea of your basic retirement financials. You should have a balance sheet listing your necessary expenses, those on which you need to survive and stay out of jail, as well as a menu of benefit payout options from Social Security and any pensions you have.

So, how do they look? Do you have enough income to cover your expenses or will you need to make adjustments? Do you see any places you can make changes?

Income from pensions and Social Security benefits, once you've made your choices, will not change. There probably will be cost-of-living adjustments, but these adjustments really don't give you more money; they just give your existing money a little more spending power. Think of it this way: If a loaf of bread costs three dollars, you receive three dollars in income. Two years from now, that same loaf of bread costs three-fifty and your income has adjusted to three-fifty. You are not receiving extra money—all you get is enough to buy the same loaf of bread.

If you won't have enough income from a pension and Social Security benefits to cover your basic needs, sit down and have a frank discussion, with your partner, about your plans. You really have two options:

1) Reduce your expenses
2) Increase your spendable income

First, take a look at your spending. Have you put together a true list of necessary living costs or have you snuck in some discretionary expenses you think you just have to have? Expenses like housing, food, and insurance are usually fixed and offer very little flexibility. However, if you have debt—especially personal debt, like credit cards and loans—this is the time to eliminate it, before you retire. Even if you must make a few sacrifices and tighten your belt the last couple of years of work, it will be to your benefit. Every dollar by which you reduce your bills each month increases your income by a dollar.

There are several ways to increase your income. The obvious one is to either continue working at your existing job or start a new career. This income could supplement your other income sources or allow you to delay taking other benefits for a larger payout later. Continuing to work might also allow you to delay accessing savings you had planned to use to supplement retirement. The longer you can avoid accessing your savings accounts, the more potential for the account to grow.

Savings vs. Income

If you're unable to work or have no desire to—but want to stay out of jail or a homeless shelter—you may use your savings accounts to supplement income.

Savings accounts are different from income benefits. When I talk about savings, I'm including all lump-sum assets you've accumulated that aren't paying you a guaranteed stream of income. In this group are non-retirement savings accounts, brokerage accounts, mutual funds, annuities, IRAs, a 401(k), and any other plans that aren't currently providing a regular income.

One of the main differences between income benefits and savings accounts is that income streams usually pay a specified benefit at a determined interval for a specified period. Your pension will pay out a benefit for the period you have chosen, single life or joint life. Social Security will do the same, for your lifetime. The benefit you receive comes with a guarantee because the pool of money to draw from already exists to provide this benefit. (There could be arguments made against Social Security or the pension system, but just understand the concept at this time.)

Savings accounts have no guarantee of a benefit. Some products will guarantee your account value against loss but not against spending. The only thing you're sure of is the account balance at a specific moment. You have full access to the account and can spend it down to zero whenever you want; when it's gone, it's gone. The upside is that unlike the income benefit provided by Social Security and pensions, which provide no potential for growth, you can invest savings accounts in any number of ways for the possibility of higher returns. They also have flexible withdrawal privileges. Usually lump sums of any amount are available at any time, depending on the product. You also have to be aware that withdrawal from retirement savings accounts may create tax liabilities and penalties; you may want to consult your tax adviser about this.

Savings accounts—whether you manage them yourself or you work with a financial adviser—are ultimately your responsibility. When you retire, your ability to add money to savings will decrease. Most of the increases in value to these accounts will come from the growth strategies you employ.

How you grow savings and the withdrawal rate will have a direct impact on how long a savings account will last. If you invest in the markets through mutual funds, stocks, and bonds, you have the potential for stronger growth but also the possibility of a prolonged downturn deflating your account. If you opt for the ultraconservative approach, you may find that your account is not earning enough to keep up with the cost of living.

Withdrawing money at too high a rate will accelerate an account's depletion. Most experts are putting the safe withdrawal rate at around 4 percent annually. If you take out more than you're earning each year, it will be necessary to take out a higher percentage the following year just to stay even. Seeing your savings erode and no way to stop it can lead to some bad strategy decisions.

Timing of your withdrawals—especially substantial amounts in the early years—can have a huge impact on later values. Large outflows and mediocre or negative returns can create a situation that results in deficits that offer little or zero chance of recovery.

The amount you've saved for retirement is often misleading. For many of us it will be the largest amount of money we've ever accumulated. If you're still working and earning a paycheck, you may be confident that you've done a good job saving. However, take away that paycheck and replace it with an income stream that barely covers or, even worse, does not cover your living expenses. Include a twenty-to-thirty-year life expectancy and all of a sudden you won't feel so confident.

Planning for using a savings account through retirement is even more complex than planning for receiving income. Remember, your income values have already been determined. You know what your Social Security benefit will be at each milestone. You know what your pension benefits are depending on the payout option you select. You make a choice from several factors and it continues for life.

Your savings accounts' future values are unknown. You may have it invested in the stock market, and values will change constantly—daily or even minute to minute. You may choose to invest in CDs or fixed income accounts and each time they mature it will be at a new rate, higher or lower than the last.

Because of the unknowns, it's important to create a strategy, once again, based on your goals and needs. Consider how your savings accounts will supplement income sources. Will you be making lump-sum withdrawals annually or will you need to convert part of your savings to an income stream? Will your withdrawals be for a set amount or will they be variable?

On the growth side, determine how much risk you can handle to get a certain rate of return. Do you know what your risk tolerance is? Are you a stock investor when the market is hot and a CD saver when it goes down? Do you work with a planner who understands your goals and your situation or do you chase the hot returns?

One scenario that could have a major negative impact on your savings account is drawing off investments during a down market. Imagine the result if you need to draw 5 percent to live on and your account is losing an additional 10 percent or more due to market returns. A couple of years like this and you could create a situation from which you would not recover. As your account shrinks, you'll need to draw a higher percentage to achieve the same dollars. As your draw becomes a higher percentage of your total, you'll need to receive a higher return to break even or take a higher percentage of principle.

Panicking during volatile times can cause you to make bad decisions. I usually see them go two ways. Some people will realize their portfolio is deteriorating and feel the only option is to swing for the fences and chase the hot returns. They disband their asset allocation strategy, forget about diversification and balance, and ignore their stated risk tolerance. They base their investments on anything that appears to be working at that moment. Their strategy changes every time they read another article or hear about a supposedly hot investment. This desperate recovery strategy tends to create volatile portfolios that show occasional short-term glimmers of hope, but the volatility just makes a bad situation worse.

The other group of people go the opposite way. They see the effect of withdrawals and a down market on their portfolio and they panic. They're like turtles—they pull everything into a shell of 100 percent safety. These people abandon their strategy by becoming super conservative and safe. They put their money in low-paying CDs and savings accounts, eliminating all risk in their portfolios, and remain there forever. Higher prices and rising inflation will erode the purchasing power of the fixed-rate savings vehicles. It will be necessary to use more principle to make up the difference for the low rate of return.

Interest rates are also variable. Some products, like money market accounts, may change weekly; CD and fixed income investments like bonds offer a fixed rate for a certain term. At the end of the term, the rates will be reissued, higher or lower.

One of the strategies I recommend to clients when using saving assets to supplement income needs is to decide how they want this money to work for them. Some people want access to cash but don't need a set income. They may need money only for specific expenses that they can't cover from their other income sources. Taking two or three years of these anticipated expenses at a time and using a money market account and laddering CD maturities to match the need works well. As they use this money, they can go back to their portfolio, draw another two or three years' worth, and start over.

You might prefer a disciplined type of payout that creates a steady, predictable income. A strategy that works nicely for this situation is to set aside three to five years of anticipated income and create a scheduled, dependable income stream. This will give you a payout for a set period, and at the end of that time, you can consider your expenses for the next five years and adjust the payout to match your new needs.

One of the reasons I prefer this carve-out and back-fill strategy is that it gives us some control as to when we take money out of our portfolios. By taking out three to five years' worth of expenses and delivering them in an income stream, you no longer have to worry about drawing off investments during a down market. If during your payout period you experience a downturn, the payouts and reserve you've established give you the opportunity to enable the markets to recover before you access them again.

Another advantage of this strategy is that it gives us the opportunity to move money out of the markets when we want. If during the five-year period we experience a huge run-up in values, we can start to sandbag a portion of this money for the next income segment.

Think back over the last several years. What if you had annuitized a five-year monthly payout in 1999 when the markets were roaring? In 2000, 2001, and 2002 the markets went through some ugly times. The markets were down double-digit percents those years. In 2003 we saw the markets start to recover, and 2004 was also a positive year.

What do you think your portfolio would look like if on top of some huge negative numbers in the stock market, you were also drawing it down at a 5 percent rate? How long do you think it would take to recover?

If you're not an experienced investor, sit down with a financial planner and discuss strategy. Even if you like to pick your own investments, a planner can illustrate various scenarios based on historical data, explain the different products, show you how they fit in to your strategy, review them, and follow up with you once you implement your strategy. Most important is that the adviser will design a plan based on the needs and goals of your own unique situation, not someone else's.

Review

- Income is a set payment for a specified period. It will not run out; the money has already been set aside to guarantee those payouts. Most payout options provide through your lifetime and that of a survivor.

- Savings have no guarantees. Values often change daily. You can deplete those accounts to zero. You can't be sure how long they'll last. When selecting an income option, consider the surviving spouse. If you opt for the large lifetime payouts, these will end at your death. Make sure you have a strategy that will provide an adequate income for the survivor.

- When setting up a strategy for your savings and investment accounts, base it on your own needs and goals, not on some-one else's. Your neighbor's aggressive investment strategy may work for her but may not be appropriate for your needs.

- Understand the types of accounts you have and the tax issues you may encounter when making withdrawals. If you received a tax break, either a deduction or deferral when you put money in, you'll pay taxes on it when you take it out.

- Create income streams to provide a steady income. This will enable you to ride out bad markets without having to draw from a depreciating portfolio.

Lifestyle Expenses

At this point I'm hoping that a number of you have had a bit of an eye opening, that you're thinking or rethinking what retirement might be like and taking a hard look at your assets and resources. It may seem like I've been spending too much time stressing the boring, serious issues, but you must understand what you'll be up against once you leave the financial security of a regular paycheck.

Your lifestyle revolves around the knowledge that every week or two weeks you receive a paycheck. Based on the amount of money you received, you sheltered and supported your family and yourself. You helped to pay for school, you entertained yourselves, traveled, and even managed to save money for retirement. You didn't get a paycheck because you were a nice person: you earned it! You went to work, did the job you were assigned, participated in your employer's growth and profitability, and in return were paid for your services.

Now, as you get ready for retirement, accept the fact that the regular paycheck that you've built your life around will be gone. You'll probably receive less than you've been accustomed to living on. If you want to enjoy the same lifestyle, you must make adjustments. You have to plan for your lifestyle expenses the same way you did for those essential expenses.

Over the years, I've met with clients on the verge of retiring who look at the value of their retirement savings account and their first thought is, How do I spend this? They want to buy a second home, travel, or give it away all without any consideration of their ability to survive.

When I was in my twenties, I worked with a couple of buddies at a manufacturing plant. Every Friday at noon we got our paychecks and immediately began making plans for the weekend. We had money in our pocket and it was party time. I didn't worry about my bills or about feeding myself later in the week. The only thing that mattered was I had some money and could afford some fun.

Monday morning would come and I'd grab my wallet and see what I had left, usually about twelve dollars. Only then would it dawn on me that I'd be eating many boxes of macaroni and cheese or cans of tuna to get by that week.

You can't look at your retirement that way—lifestyle first, necessary bills last. It has to be the other way around. The advantage for me was I knew I'd get another check in five days (and macaroni and cheese was one of my favorite foods). For you, in retirement, if you spend down your savings too quickly, you may not have the resources to build it back up.

This is why I put the emphasis on making sure you always have those essential expenses paid as a top priority. Assume you cover your necessary expenses and you have some money left over; now we can talk about lifestyle expenses.

Your lifestyle expenses are those that create the life you choose to live. They're the costs for your daily activities, your recreation, and even your personal development. Sometimes there's a thin line between certain necessary and lifestyle expenses, but for the most part, lifestyle expenses tend to be discretionary and flexible. Just as with necessary expenses, use a budget or a spreadsheet to determine how much you expect to spend each week and where the money will come from. Do you want to play golf once a week? Do you want to have dinner out with friends or go to the movies? Plan it, see how these activities fit in to your budget. For large expenses like travel, give yourself plenty of time to prepare for the cost and understand what impact it'll have on your savings and income.

Be careful when considering where the money will come from for your lifestyle expenses. Don't sacrifice essential expenses for a lifestyle expense. Remember, these are necessary expenses because you need them to survive or there's a commitment with negative consequences if you don't pay. Don't skip a payment for a critical bill to go out for dinner with friends. You'll dig a hole you can't get out of and will create a pattern of payment problems.

Also, don't rack up credit card debt with the idea of carrying it indefinitely. It might seem like a great idea to charge a five-thousand-dollar vacation on your credit card, thinking, "It's only a hundred dollars a month." That one hundred dollars a month will go on forever and is a hundred dollars you won't have each month to cover your expenses. So think before you spend.

If you have difficulty funding those necessary expenses and all the activities you want, consider working part time to pay for them. I know people who work for six to nine months a year to pay for their winter vacation in Florida. I have a client who wants to play golf three times a week and works as a starter at a golf course. A friend is working part time at a local college and receives discounts for some courses.

Some of you will have enough savings and income to go out and enjoy your retirement without too many concerns. You're the ones who planned for retirement long before it got here and were able to take the proper steps. Others for one reason or another weren't able to prepare as well. Those who didn't plan as well will have to be a bit more cautious with their lifestyle expenses. You'll have to plan a little harder and find other ways to fund your dreams, but this doesn't mean you have to give up on them.

Review

- Lifestyle expenses are for activities that are important to you as an individual but not necessary for your survival.

- You must satisfy your survival expenses before your lifestyle expenses.

- Consider activities that are free, such as walking, hiking, reading, a day at the beach, picnics, visiting, volunteering your time, gardening, writing, and fishing.

- Look for discounts and non-peak specials for travel. A flexible schedule is one advantage of retirement.

Money for Other Purposes

Up until now, we've looked at how money will fund your retirement. We talked about necessary monthly expenses and the importance of prioritizing these, and lifestyle expenses and how to plan for them. We've looked at the differences between income sources and savings accounts.

We've looked at how your money fits into your life and how it will provide for you. This is great: Your money that you've worked hard for should feed and entertain you as you begin to move away from a regular paycheck. You should feel good that you've made it to where you can consider retiring. As I've told my mother on many occasions, "You and Dad worked for your money. I hope you're able to spend every penny of it." (She keeps telling me she's trying.)

When talking to clients about their retirement plans, most are looking forward to enjoying their time and their money. As we delve into their goals, plans, and dreams, I find that many want to go beyond their own needs and enjoyment. They talk about how important it is to make sure their children receive enough money to get them started with their own families. They want to make sure there's money to pay for their grandchildren's college bills. They want to help their church, give to their alumni funds, or support a cause. Each of you will have a different reason and your own priority for satisfying this dream.

These goals require the same kind of planning and thought you gave to your necessary expenses and lifestyle expenses, but with a few twists. The first thing to remember again is you cannot sacrifice your ability to meet your necessary expenses to give to others. Your survival is most important. If you want to sacrifice a discretionary lifestyle expense and use your money for other purposes, that's fine. That's your personal priority.

Some considerations are:

- When and how do you want to pass the assets on to another person or entity?

- Do you want to make annual gifts or will you make a substantial one-time contribution?

- Will the asset be available immediately? Do you want it for future use?

- Will you make the gift during your lifetime or after your death?

- Will it be cash, a security, or property?

If you want to give a grandchild money to help pay for current college bills while you're still alive, providing cash or paying the bill directly can accomplish this goal. If you want to pay for a child's education eighteen years down the road, a 529 savings plan might be a better way to fund that goal.

Life insurance is an ideal way to leave a cash benefit after death. Life insurance can leverage premium dollars into hundreds or thousands of death-benefit dollars. It can allow you to leave a substantial amount of money without reducing your current assets. Beneficiaries can be named recipients of the policy, and they can be people or charities or trusts.

If you're passing assets at death, you may want to use a will or a trust to designate where, when, and to whom they will go. An attorney will be necessary to draft these documents but this will help you control your assets even after you've passed.

Gifting money to certain organizations during life or at death can satisfy your charitable goals and may even provide you with certain tax deductions and advantages.

You and your spouse will have your own reasons and your priorities concerning these assets. They may be as simple as putting a ten-dollar bill in a birthday card or as complex as dividing a large estate with multiple beneficiaries.

Gifting can be tricky when trying to coordinate your wishes with your assets. Sit down with a financial planner or attorney or CPA for more complex issues to determine the best strategy for your wishes.

WORKSHEET

How does gifting fit into your retirement planning?

What are your priorities for gifting?

Will gifts be made during your lifetime or after your death?

What are the tax strategies for your gifting?

In what forms will gifts be?

4

Bumps in the Road

Preparing for the Unexpected

The idea behind this book is for you to be ready for retirement before it happens. The first section was about creating your retirement dream. This is the section in which you list all the things you have wanted to do and all the places you've wanted to go. This is where you list all of your daydreams and visualize your day-to-day lifestyle.

Next, we do more of the nuts-and-bolts planning. This is where you assess your finances—that is, look at your expenses and cash flow. This is where you start thinking about Social Security, pensions, and savings, where you start to separate and prioritize basic living expenses and lifestyle expenses and think about money for other purposes.

This is the "what-if" section. There are two possibilities. "What if" everything goes as planned? You and your spouse prepared for your retirement and you now live your lives to the fullest. Then I hope you say, "It's a good thing we read Mike's book twenty years ago to get us ready for retirement." I'm rooting for you all the way.

The other "what-if" possibility is that life will not go as planned. "What if" you or your spouse has a health issue that requires long-term care? "What if" you haven't planned properly for your estate to transfer to your beneficiaries?

Retirement Readiness means being prepared, going into retirement with a plan for both the good times and any twists and turns along the way. Every goal that's accomplished has a well-thought-out plan of action and a way to handle obstacles. Your plan for retirement and for the goals you want to have accomplished after you're gone needs to have a strategy to deal with obstacles.

WORKSHEET

What are the obstacles that may prevent you from enjoying the retirement of your dreams?

How are you preparing to deal with them?

Health

I've had hundreds of conversations over the years with people concerning their plans for their current or upcoming retirement life. In almost all of the talks, when discussing how they want to live, I hear the same phrase over and over: "as long as my health holds out." "I want to keep working as long as my health holds out." "We want to travel as long as our health holds out."

Your health—the way you feel and the way your body ages—will have a tremendous impact on the way you spend your retirement years. It will allow you to enjoy an active life or force you to lead a more sedentary existence.

So many things have affected our health over the last fifty or sixty years, some we could have controlled and some over which we had no control. Diet, exercise, smoking, drinking were choices and could have been controlled. However, twenty or thirty years ago, there was little consideration of how these habits would affect us as we got older. Now we're learning how our eating habits, regular exercise, moderation with alcohol, and giving up tobacco can improve our health and quality of life.

Diabetes, cancer, and heart problems that even two decades ago were "kiss-of-death" diagnoses are now beatable or at least controllable.

Of course you can't repair the wear and tear of a lifetime of bad habits by eating a few vegetables, taking a handful of vitamins, and walking around the block. You need to work with your doctor, do some research on your own, and make a commitment to take care of yourself, not just for you but also for those who depend on and care for you.

But even though you eat right, exercise, and follow your doctor's instructions, as the saying goes, "Stuff happens," and when stuff happens, you need to be prepared and understand how to deal with it. You need to be prepared to deal with health issues physically and financially. You need to understand where the money will come from to cover the cost of medical treatment. You need to understand what's covered and what costs are your responsibility.

Medicare

Medicare is a federal health insurance program available to people age sixty-five and older. President Lyndon Johnson signed the bill into law in 1965. (Do not confuse it with Medicaid, which provides benefits to low-income people.)

Medicare receives its funding through payroll taxes; 2.9 percent of your earnings go to pay for your Medicare benefits. If you have an employer, each of you will contribute 1.4 percent; if you're self-employed, you'll contribute the full amount.

You become eligible for Medicare on the first day of the month that you turn sixty-five. If you're eligible for Social Security, you'll automatically be enrolled in Medicare Parts A and B. If you choose not to participate in Part B, you must actively decline the option. You'll receive your Medicare card three months before your sixty-fifth birthday. Your spouse can enroll in Medicare Part A when he or she is sixty-five, based on your work record, even if you're between sixty-two and sixty-four years old.

Even though you've been contributing to Medicare benefits with each paycheck,nd it's not free. It has copays, premiums, and deductibles. Estimates are that a retiree will need $250,000 and up to pay Medicare premiums, deductibles, copayments, and uncovered drug costs. If long-term care becomes necessary, that will add to the cost.

The effect health care will have on retirement is considerable; therefore, it's important that you have an understanding of what Medicare does and does not cover before you reach age sixty-five and must depend on it.

Medicare comes in four parts, A, B, C, and D. Parts A and B are the original Medicare plan. Part C, also known as the Medicare Advantage Plan, is a private-sector, managed-care plan. Part D is a new benefit for prescription drugs.

The Original Recipe

Parts A, B, and Medigap

Medicare Part A covers care in hospitals and skilled nursing facilities. It's subject to deductibles and copays that adjust annually. In 2007, there was a $992 deductible for the first sixty days of hospitalization, $248 per day for days sixty-one through ninety, and $496 per day for up to an additional sixty days. After being discharged for sixty days, if you're readmitted, you must start a new cycle of charges for the deductible and daily costs.

Care in skilled nursing facilities is less expensive. Medicare covers the first twenty days of care; days twenty-one through one hundred have a copay of $124 per day. After one hundred days, the patient pays 100 percent of the cost.

Medicare Part B covers outpatient care, doctor visits, lab tests, and supplies and equipment. Part B has been adding coverage to include preventive care, including mammograms and glaucoma screenings. You automatically enroll in Part B when you became eligible for Part A, but you have the option to decline.

To receive Part B coverage, you must pay a premium. Starting in 2007, the premium for Part B is based on a sliding scale depending on income. Those individuals earning less than $80,000 annually will pay $93.50 per month. Individuals whose income is greater than $80,000 per year (modified adjusted gross income) and couples whose income is greater than $160,000 per year will pay a higher premium that maxes out at $161.40 per individual. Beneficiaries of Part B also pay a 20 percent coinsurance fee.

Looking at the out-of-pocket expenses that come with Medicare, it's easy to see why most retirees supplement their coverage with a Medigap policy. Medigap is a private insurance plan with twelve standardized variations per state. It's available to fill the "gaps" to help cover your costs over what Medicare will pay. You must currently participate in Part A and Part B. Most Medigap plans cover hospital coinsurance, a percentage of physician fees, and other outpatient services.

Medigap works only with the Original Medicare Plan, and both you and your spouse need your own individual coverage.

Compare policies—the benefits and standard costs can vary among insurance companies.

Medicare Advantage Plans
Part C

Medicare Advantage Plans are plans similar to the HMOs and PPOs you were part of while employed. To qualify, you must enroll in Medicare Parts A and B, pay the Part B premium, and live within the plan's service area.

These plans often have networks, which means you may have to give up your current doctor and use one that belongs to the plan and go to certain hospitals. Some plans will require a referral to a specialist and others don't require a referral but have an additional charge to go outside the network.

Medicare pays the network of hospitals, doctors, and other health care providers a monthly fee, whether or not you use the service. Your cost will depend on the type of plan and availability in your area.

These plans will cover all services provided by the Original Medicare Plan and may cover some additional services, including Part D drug coverage. They also might reduce out-of-pocket expenses.

Drug Coverage
Part D

In 2006, Medicare launched Part D, outpatient prescription drug benefits. Private companies offer these plans and enrollment is voluntary. You must have Medicare Part A and Part B to qualify. Most plans charge a premium in addition to your Part B premium.

Whether to enroll in Part D requires some real thought. The following example shows a plan based on 2007 Medicare standards. You'll pay a $32 (approximate) monthly premium not included in your out-of-pocket requirements, and a $265 annual deductible. Then you pay 25 percent and your plan pays 75 percent of your annual drug costs until you reach $2,400. From $2,400 until you hit

$3,850 in out-of-pocket expenses, there is no coverage. This gap is the "doughnut hole"—during this time you pay 100 percent of all prescription costs, and you continue to pay any monthly premiums. Once you've reached the $3,850 level of expense, you pay a coinsurance 5 percent for the rest of the year.

Before enrolling in Part D, make sure it will work to your advantage. Compare it to a Medicare advantage plan, and Medigap coverage, or see what alternative programs you may qualify for and which one is the most advantageous to you.

WORKSHEET

Go to *www.medicare.gov* to learn more about your Medicare options.

Will you have any retiree medical benefits from your employer or union?

Did you serve in the military? If so, contact the Veterans Administration to see if you qualify for benefits.

Long-Term Care

The good news is that our generation has a longer life expectancy than that of previous ones. The bad news is that not all of us will live our extra years healthy, active, and mentally sharp. Some of us could spend years in declining health, depending on other people to help us perform the most basic tasks—activities like eating, bathing, dressing, and using the bathroom. Physical or mental illness can strike anyone at any age, but as we get older, we become more vulnerable.

As the 78 million baby boomers start to age, the federal government has estimated about 60 percent of them will need some kind of long-term care. The question is: If you're one of those who need the care, who will provide it?

Over the years, as I have talked to pre-retirees and new retirees, the discussion of long-term care has been one of the more difficult subjects. One reason is everyone knows someone, a parent or grandparent, brother or a sister, who has been dependent on others for long-term care and help. Sometimes it's temporary and the people recover and resume their normal lives. Sometimes it's an end-of-life situation or there's no chance for recovery.

In most cases, family members take care of us. They do what they can within their limits, giving up their own time to help the people who helped them.

I think it's an important conversation, because people know it could easily be themselves at some point depending on others for care. Some have experienced the stress and demands of 24/7 care to a family member. It can be physically and emotionally draining.

It can also require a tremendous drain on finances when the family is no longer able to provide the necessary care. The cost of extended care in a private nursing home can easily be in excess of $7,000 per month. Considering a three-to-five-year stay, you're looking at a large outlay of cash. Even the cost of skilled in-home care is often well over one hundred dollars a day.

Unless you have the assets that can absorb that kind of cost without affecting your plans, you need to think this over. As you just learned, Medicare will give you the first twenty days free and the coinsurance is $124 per day for days twenty-one to one hundred. After that, the patient is responsible for 100 percent.

So how can you prepare for the possibility that you or your spouse will need long-term care?

One way is to self-insure, but as we just discussed, it probably isn't practical for most of us. Another way is to gather your family members and have them promise that they'll take care of you, no matter what. Once again, this is not a practical strategy; it may not even be what you'd want.

Another option is to purchase insurance to guard against the costs of long-term care. Long-term care insurance is one of the most underutilized financial tools. Everyone seems to understand the possibilities and outcomes of not preparing for the need of extended care, but that's where the conversation ends.

The idea of long-term care insurance makes as much sense as car insurance. We insure our cars against the possibility that we'll be in an accident; we do not plan on the accident but have the insurance just in case. The insurance is there to cover the cost to replace our car, to pay hospital bills for others and ourselves, and to protect us against lawsuits. All of these could have been financially disastrous if we hadn't protected ourselves through the purchase of insurance.

Long-term care insurance will provide you with a benefit to pay for costs if you're required to stay in a healthcare facility. It can also provide you with money for in-home care. Policies are determined by costs and desired benefits.

Long-term care insurance is best purchased while we're young and still in good health. As we get older and start to develop health problems, our insurance premiums will increase and getting a policy issued will be more difficult. In 2006, 42 percent of applications for clients aged seventy to seventy-nine were declined.

It is important to understand some of the basic parts of an LTC policy, and how they affect the policy.

- The *elimination period* is how long you have to wait before coverage begins. It is usually 0, 30, 60, 90, or 180 days. The shorter the elimination period, the more expensive the policy. If you choose the longer period, it is important to consider how you'll pay for your care during that time. Remember, Medicare will offer some coverage for one hundred days.

- The *benefit period* is how long you'll receive benefits. Periods can be two, three, five, ten years, even a lifetime. The longer the benefit period, the more expensive the policy.

- The *benefit amount* is where you determine how much cash benefit you'd like to receive from your policy. Benefits are usually based on a daily amount from fifty dollars to five hundred dollars per day.

- *Inflation options* are contained in the most important rider in an LTC policy. What this rider does is raise your daily benefit to keep it in line with increases in LTC costs. If you're young and don't plan on using your policy for twenty or thirty years, your benefits will not have the purchasing power they have now.

- *Joint spousal coverage* can offer discounts and may allow spouses to share benefits at their discretion.

Just like the other concepts we've discussed here, LTC may or may not be right for you. It's something you need to look at within the framework of your situation. It's also something that you should discuss with a financial planner who you feel can help direct you the right way.

Power of Attorney

At some point, you may decide to give an individual authority to act on your behalf. It may be because you're away from home and a decision has to be made immediately—maybe a contract with a contractor or it becomes necessary to sign a check from your account in your absence. As we age and our ability or enthusiasm to go to the bank or deal with business or legal activity wanes, we may decide to give a trusted person the authority to act as our agent on our behalf.

Usually a power of attorney, drafted by a lawyer, outlines what powers and under what conditions your agent (or attorney-in-fact) may act on your behalf. Powers can be confined to one act or type of act or apply to all activities. Powers can also be durable: They will continue to be effective even if you become incapacitated. However, a power of attorney ends at death regardless of the type.

The agent must be honest in all his or her dealings on your behalf. The power is revocable—that is, it may be withdrawn. It's important to realize that third parties with whom the agent exercised authority in the past may not realize that the power has been revoked. If the power is revoked, notify those third parties immediately.

Durable Power of Attorney for Health Care and Living Wills

A durable power of attorney for health care (DPOAHC) is similar to a durable power of attorney because you're appointing someone to make decisions on your behalf. The difference is that you're authorizing someone to make medical decisions, including whether or not to continue with life-sustaining treatments, not decisions regarding business and property.

The DPOAHC is a springing power that becomes effective upon your inability to make your healthcare decisions

A living will is a directive concerning the treatment to be taken or not taken when you are no longer able to make your own healthcare decisions.

My reason for mentioning these documents is to make you aware of them. The POA, DPOAHC, and the living will create situations where you'll be giving another person the power to make decisions concerning your finances, property, and life. Not only will you as the giver of these powers feel the responsibility of naming the person to carry them out, but also the receiver of the power has the responsibility of making your most critical decisions—including the decision to "let you go."

People are reluctant to discuss these documents because they are associated with the actual death of a person. Wills, trusts, and inheritances are easier to talk about because they'll come after the passing, when the burial is over, after loved ones have had time to catch their breath. There is no rush to settle these affairs—that can be done when everyone is ready.

But these other documents are assigning end-of-life powers to someone, and when the decision is made, it goes into effect now. Even though it will make sense and is the right thing to do, the choice that was made might be carried around for a long time.

The assignment of these powers will require many conversations with those family members and others who will be involved. Your attorney will be involved to make sure the documents are properly drafted and to help guide you in the correct direction.

5

Make Sure It Goes Where You Want It to Go

Preparing Your Estate

E state planning is simply making sure your assets go where you want them to when you're gone. It's the strategy that you create, while alive, to make sure your beneficiaries receive your assets in the most tax-and-time-efficient way. Your estate is everything you own: cash, bank accounts, investments, property, cars, jewelry, your home, and so on.

Estate planning, like all the other planning we've discussed, is a process that requires adequate thought regardless of the size of your estate. If you have specific desires for its distribution, it's critical that you document them. Don't let your beneficiaries fight over or guess who was to get what. It's even more important that you not die without documentation or instructions—or the courts will decide who'll receive your assets. Your estate plan should allow for the distribution of your estate to which beneficiaries, and what portion or particular items you want them to receive. Even when and under what conditions they receive their inheritance can be included in your estate plan. Make sure your plan stays current with your wishes. Relationships over time can change, and if they do, you need to make sure you adjust your plan accordingly.

An estate plan should also consider the effects of taxes to the beneficiaries and the estate itself. Federal estate taxes and income tax on certain accounts can take a big chunk of inheritance money intended for other purposes. Proper planning and strategy can offset or avoid some of these taxes and preserve the estate for the beneficiaries.

Your estate strategy should allow your assets to pass quickly. *Probate* is the legal process that settles claims and distributes an estate, but it can be a long and costly process. By using strategies that avoid probate and pass assets directly to your beneficiaries, you can cut down on time and settlement costs.

Estate planning can be as simple as naming a joint owner or as complex as multigenerational trusts and beneficiaries. As you consider the creation of an estate plan, make sure you consult with a financial adviser, a tax adviser, and an attorney. They are the ones who can make sure your strategy aligns with your goals.

Probate, Intestacy, and Wills

Some of you are probably familiar with probate and wills through your own experiences. You may have been named in a will to receive an inheritance from a family member or a close friend. This is one way of passing along assets at death so let's take a look at the process.

Anyone over the age of majority can draft his or her own will. An attorney is not necessary, but employing one is highly advisable; remember, you won't be around to clarify any confusion. If you worded something wrong or left something out, it will be too late to correct it (after all, you'll be gone).

The person who makes the will is called the *testator,* and the will transfers assets according to the testator's instruction at his or her death. This occurs through the probate process, but not all assets are transferred this way. *Beneficiaries, joint tenant with right of survivorship,* and assets held in a *trust* prevail over the will and do not go through probate. These are called *will substitutes.*

A person who dies with a *valid will* is said to have died *testate*. Sometimes a person will have assets that are not named in the will and are not covered by any other method of transfer. Not having these assets named is called *intestacy*. In this case, the courts will decide, according to the state laws of intestacy, who will receive the property. To avoid this, most wills contain a clause, known as the *residuary clause* that universally includes all assets not individually named.

Wills are not irrevocable—that is, they can be changed or amended by a document referred to as a *codicil*. A will can also be revoked by physically destroying it. It's important to have new documentation in place before destroying the old will in case of an unexpected death. With the old will destroyed and no new documentation, the estate will pass by the laws of intestacy.

Probate is the actual legal process of administering an estate. First, the judge of the probate court will determine the validity of the will. Next, the court appoints someone to represent and manage the probate estate. If the personal representative is the person named in the will, he or she is called the *executor* or *executrix*. If the court appoints someone, that person is the *administrator*. It's up to this person to inventory and collect the deceased's property, pay any debts and outstanding taxes, and distribute the remaining property according to the instructions of the will.

Probate can take several months and can carry substantial court costs and attorney's fees to complete the administration.

Those who die without a valid will and don't hold their property in a will substitute form are considered *intestate*. The disposition of their property is then via the probate court through the laws of intestacy. The laws vary from state to state but their primary concern is to provide for the surviving spouse and family members. The laws don't allow for distribution to charities or non-family members. If there are no heirs or beneficiaries that fall under the state's laws, the property will be held by the state for a period of time. If at the end of that time no long-forgotten family member comes forth or a valid will is found, the property goes to the state.

There are numerous disadvantages of intestacy. Shares distributed are fixed with no regard to age, need, or concerns. The laws follow bloodlines, so there's no way to benefit friends, charities, stepchildren and with a few state exceptions, domestic partners. There is no consideration of tax strategies if the problem exists.

Remember, if you own assets at your death, you have an estate, and you should have a strategy to make sure that your assets get passed on the way you planned.

WORKSHEET

How will you transfer your estate at your death?

When was the last time you sat down and reviewed your will to make sure it carried out your current wishes?

Are there any assets not covered by your estate strategy? What are they?

Ownership and Beneficiaries

How you own assets often determines how these assets transfer at death. There are two ways you own assets: alone (*individual ownership*) and with others (*joint ownership*).

Items owned individually transfer according to the directions of your estate plan. If you're using a will, they transfer through the probate process; some assets will allow the naming of a beneficiary; or you may title them in a trust. The key is to direct these assets to where you want them to go upon your death.

Joint ownership has two common designations. The most common is *joint tenant with right of survivorship*. Most couples own the bulk of their assets in this manner, though the joint owners need not be married. Both own the assets equally while alive and at the death of the first owner the survivor owns the assets completely.

Joint tenant with right of survivor avoids probate and may seem like a simple solution, but it does carry some significant disadvantages. Once a person is named a joint owner, you can't remove him or her without that person's permission. This may not be an issue between you and your spouse, but it is a consideration. In addition, the surviving spouse must have a plan for passing the assets at his or her death, and both spouses must have a contingency plan in the event of simultaneous death. A third downside is the possible loss of use of the estate tax exemption, a credit to reduce your taxable estate and therefore your possible tax liability. This will be discussed under Death and Taxes (page 85).

Joint tenants in common allows for joint ownership in unequal shares. It also enables each owner to name his own beneficiaries at his death. The decedent's shares don't go to the surviving owners, but instead to the decedent's estate, via his will, which will be probated. *This type of ownership is not considered a will substitute.*

Whereas owners have direct control of an asset during life, for our purposes a *beneficiary* has no connection until she receives it at the death of an owner. It's not her asset until then. Beneficiaries are usually named on life insurance, annuities, retirement plans, and trusts. Their benefits bypass probate; they are received directly, according to the instructions of the decedent. They may carry tax liabilities (later). Beneficiary designations are revocable unless stated otherwise and they can be people, entities, trusts, charities and even pets.

Most bank and brokerage accounts can also carry beneficiary designations without requiring a joint owner. *Payable on death (POD)* accounts, held at financial institutions, will be paid to a beneficiary, at death, avoiding probate. The owner has complete control of the assets throughout his life and the beneficiary has no access to the account until the death of the owner. *Totten trusts (ITF)* are also used by banks and work the same way. If you have brokerage accounts, the *transfer on death (TOD)* account accomplishes the same goals. All of these designations, unless specified, are revocable.

Beneficiary designations, like all estate paperwork, should be reviewed every few years to make sure they match your current goals. Things like life insurance, IRAs, and annuities may have been opened years ago when your life and the people in it were different. Imagine the disaster when your spouse discovers that the million-dollar life insurance policy you bought twenty-five years ago names your ex-wife as beneficiary.

It is important to note that assets held in joint ownership or that are received by a beneficiary are included in the estate, for estate tax calculations, unless specifically removed by gifting or the use of an irrevocable trust.

When reviewing beneficiaries, request a copy of the document from your bank or custodian and keep it in a safe place along with all other important documents.

Make sure someone else knows where these documents are and how to access them if something happens to you.

If you have had changes in your relationships and beneficiaries have to be changed, it's up to you to do it. Don't assume that your divorce paperwork or the fact that you changed your will covers changes in beneficiaries. Beneficiaries prevail over other documentation. If you eliminate an ex-spouse from your will but leave him as beneficiary on your life insurance or an annuity, guess what? He'll get the money!

Trusts

To some of us, the idea of owning a trust brings back storylines at the Sunday-afternoon movies we watched as kids. The snooty, well-to-do family didn't work but received a hefty allowance from a trust fund set up by a deceased relative, and rubbed everyone's nose in it. It's true that trusts can be set up to create this exact scenario. However, they do come in a variety of shapes, sizes, and names that can be valuable planning tools for both large estates and those not-so-large ones.

Trusts are created to direct the disposition of assets, provide income, avoid probate, or reduce taxes. There are two basic categories, revocable and irrevocable, and from these two categories there are numerous variations. This section will give you a brief understanding of another strategy for estate planning. As I've mentioned, before you make any decisions, sit down with the experts—a financial adviser, a tax adviser, and your attorney to see which strategy best fits your needs and goals.

The *revocable living trust* has become quite popular. In this arrangement an individual shifts the ownership of property from his name to the trust. As its name implies, this trust is created and funded during an individual's life (also known as an *inter vivos trust*) and can be changed or terminated at any time.

The person creating the trust is known as the *trustor* or *grantor*. The trustor must change ownership of the items held in her name to ownership by another trust. If title is not changed, the item is not included in the trust. Property held in joint tenancy with right of survivorship or joint tenant in common is not owned or disbursed by the trust. Property that names a beneficiary other than the trust is not disbursed by the trust.

When the trustor creates the trust, she names a *trustee*. This person manages the trust assets according to the directions of the trust. The trustee can be the trustor, another person, or an institution. A successor trustee can be named in the event that the original trustee can no longer serve.

The *trust agreement* contains the instructions regarding the management of assets and the disposition of assets at the death of the trustor. The trust agreement may also carry instructions for the management of assets should the trustor become incompetent.

Beneficiaries can be anyone or any entity. They are named by the trustor and have no control over the trust. When they receive the assets and their share of the estate, it is determined by the trust document.

It's important to understand the advantages and confusion surrounding the revocable living trust. Because the trustor maintains control over the trust to revoke or change the terms, the trust is taxed as her asset. Revocable living trusts don't provide tax savings; income is taxed to the trustor, at her rate, and reported on her federal and state returns.

The assets are included in the trustor's estate and figure in the calculation for estate tax purposes. Assets held in the trust do not go through probate, however; the creation and management of the assets held in the trust can be costly and possibly exceed the cost of probate over time.

These assets are also considered available to pay for nursing home expenses. Once again, this is due to the control the trustor has over the assets.

Another type of trust is a *testamentary trust*. This is created at the death of the trustor. Usually the assets are directed to the trust by a *pour-over will*. The trust is the beneficiary of the will, and after probate the assets pour over into the trust.

Irrevocable trusts are similar to revocable trusts as far as leaving assets and avoiding probate. The trustor makes an irrevocable gift of the property to the trust and gives up control of the asset. The trust is irrevocable and the terms can't be changed. The trust is treated as a separate entity and pays the taxes for the income it generates. These trusts have a number of uses involving sophisticated tax and estate planning. Two common uses are reducing estates, thus controlling estate tax liabilities and removing assets from an individual's ownership to avoid future claims against them.

When considering the use of trusts for estate planning purposes, sit down with the professionals; accountant, attorney, and financial adviser. Make sure they understand what you want to accomplish, and together create the strategy that will get you there.

WORKSHEET

What do you want your estate planning to accomplish?

Who gets what?

When should they get it?

Death and Taxes

Taxes aren't going to mean a lot to you when you have passed on, but they'll mean something to those you leave behind. Taxes will reduce the amount of the estate you leave to your beneficiaries. You and your beneficiaries should carefully consider the impact taxes will have and take steps to prepare for them. If you don't, Uncle Sam could be the biggest beneficiary.

When you die, the administrator of your estate will file your final income tax returns, federal and state, for any earnings you may have, up to and including the date of death. This includes W2 wages, taxable distributions from IRAs and retirement plans, and earnings from savings, investment accounts, and any other sources. The personal representative will also file an *estate fiduciary tax return*, if you leave an estate that goes through probate or a living trust. This will be based on the income the estate earns, beginning the day after death to year's end, and will continue to be filed until the estate has been distributed. Once the estate has been distributed, the beneficiaries are responsible for reporting income from the distributed property on their own tax returns.

Not only will it be necessary for you to plan the transfer of your assets in a tax-efficient manner, but also your beneficiaries need to plan how they'll accept and use those assets, and what, if any, tax issues exist.

The most common taxable event occurs when a beneficiary inherits IRAs and retirement plans. Money withdrawn from these accounts is taxed at the beneficiary's current tax rate. There are strategies you can employ to control the taxing of these accounts. Spouses aren't required to take distributions. A surviving spouse can execute a *spousal rollover* — that is, roll the retirement account into her own without a taxable event. This maintains the tax deferral of the account and will delay taxes until the spouse makes a withdrawal based on needs or is required to at seventy and a half for required minimum distribution purposes.

A non-spouse beneficiary has two choices regarding these accounts. The first is to take a lump-sum distribution of the account and pay the taxes due. The second is to use a *stretch IRA* and take withdrawals based on her life expectancy. In order to do this, they must create a *beneficiary IRA*. The titling of the account will be, for example, Jane Smith Deceased Beneficiary IRA FBO Tom Smith. The titling of the account is crucial. The beneficiary can't name the IRA hers—it must remain in the name of the deceased. It's also important to make sure any changes of custodians be done as a direct trustee-to-trustee transfer. The beneficiary does not get the sixty-day rollover privilege. The beneficiary must begin distributions by December 31 of the year following death. The distribution is calculated on a life expectancy distribution, just like RMD, based on the beneficiary's age. The advantage of this is that the beneficiary can delay paying taxes on the lump sum—only the amount distributed is taxable.

Another way to lessen the tax load for your beneficiaries is to *convert* a *traditional IRA* to a *Roth IRA* while you're still alive. A Roth IRA will provide a spousal beneficiary with tax-free distributions, and a non-spouse can take a tax-free lump-sum distribution or stretch out tax-free distributions based on their life expectancy. You'll pay taxes on the amount you convert, but it may save dollars down the road.

The most discussed, feared, and least understood tax at death is the *federal estate tax*. This is a tax due on the total value of your estate, over certain levels. In 2007 and 2008, every person can take advantage of an *estate tax exemption* and pass $2,000,000 to their beneficiaries, before taxes are due. A married couple can pass $2,000,000 each for a total of $4,000,000. Any amounts over this would be taxed at 45 percent. In 2009, the exemption goes to $3,500,000 each, $7,000,000 per couple. In 2010, it gets weird: The estate tax goes away for one year, only to reappear in 2011. The exemption in 2011 will be $1,000,000 each, $2,000,000 per couple, with a top tax rate of 55 percent. Remember, this is the federal estate tax; your state may have a separate estate tax.

Before you can determine if you have an estate tax issue, you must know what comprises your estate. Your estate is anything you own, cash, stocks, jewelry, real estate, any other assets, and the death benefit of any life insurance you own. If you start adding it up, when the exemption drops to $1,000,000 in 2011, you may be close.

Estate taxes can be reduced by decreasing the amount of the estate you pass on. Gifting assets each year, creating irrevocable trusts, placing life insurance ownership in life insurance trusts, and taking advantage of the estate tax exemption are all ways of decreasing your estate.

The easiest and most overlooked strategy is to make sure both spouses take advantage of the exemption. A married couple can pass an unlimited amount of assets to each other without any tax liability. Because married couples usually hold assets as joint tenant with right of survivorship or name each other as primary beneficiary of assets, the full amount of the first spouse to die's assets passes directly to the surviving spouse, without taking advantage of the exemption. When the second spouse dies, the estate makes use of his or her exemption and the rest is subject to any estate taxes. Thus, the estate pays taxes on the combined estate less one deduction.

The way to make sure the first spouse to die takes advantage of the exemption is to direct the amount of the exemption to someone other than his spouse. The exemption is not automatic at the death of the first spouse; he must direct the assets. The surviving spouse will receive the remainder of the estate; upon her death the taxes will be calculated on the remaining estate less two exemptions.

This can be an easy solution. Perhaps you decide to name a child as beneficiary of assets valued up to the exemption amount. Those assets are not included in your estate for calculation of the estate tax, and the remainder of assets (if available) will pass to your surviving spouse and allow both of you to take advantage of the exemption. The downside to this solution is the beneficiary of the exemption amount now owns a considerable amount of assets that were part of the estate that may have been intended to care for the surviving spouse. What if the remaining assets are not enough for the survivor to live on? Have you created a problem by leaving the assets to someone else? Your spouse would no longer have the ability to use those assets should it become necessary.

Forethought and proper estate planning can provide solutions. The use of *A/B trusts, bypass trusts, credit shelter trusts,* and other variations allows the first spouse to die to transfer into a trust the amount of the exemption. This trust names a non-spouse as beneficiary. The amount is not included in what is transferred to the surviving spouse, and is exempted from the estate tax calculation. The big plus for this strategy is that it enables the surviving spouse to have access to the trust's principal and income for most expenses.

This is a simplified version of the concept—discuss any strategies with your team of professionals—but it should help you realize how important it is to take the time to understand the issues involved in estate planning, and ways to prepare for them.

EXAMPLE

This is one example of how proper planning can reduce tax liability and leave more money to your beneficiaries.

It is January 30, 2011, the estate tax exemption is $1,000,000, and the maximum tax rate is 55 percent. Bill and Mary have been married for twenty-five years. They have no estate plan, and have accumulated $5,000,000 in assets, split $2,500,000 each. Bill has had health issues, and passes away. All assets go directly to Mary. Five years later, Mary passes. The assumption is that she has earned 5 percent annually on the funds and that the tax exemption and rate are the same.

Bill 1/30/11	Mary 2/1/11	Estate 2/1/16
Estate $2,500,000	Estate total $5,000,000	$6,381,407
	Exemption	− $1,000,000
	Taxable estate	$5,381,407
	@55%	− $2,959,773
	To Heirs	$2,421,634

Now let's assume a Credit Shelter Trust to take advantage of Bill's exemption.

Bill 1/30/11	Mary 2/1/11	Estate 2/1/16
Estate $2,500,000	Estate total $4,000,000	$5,105,126
To Mary $1,500,000	Exemption	− $1,000,000
To CST $1,000,000	Taxable Estate	$4,105,126
	@55%	− $2,257,819
		$1,847,307
	CST @ 5 percent Earnings Annually	+ $1,276,281
	To Heirs	$3,123,588

The credit shelter trust increases the amount to the heirs by reducing the tax liability, and Mary has access to the money if she needs it without having to include it in her estate.

I'm going to repeat myself here, but when considering your estate plan, don't forget to bring in a team of experts.

Life Insurance: A Hedge

It's always good to have a hedge against things that could go wrong. A hedge is like a safety net—it may not give you full protection but it offers some protection and offsets the negatives. Life insurance can be a hedge. It provides a cash benefit that can replace lost income or used to pay the taxes and expenses that occur during the settlement of an estate. Life insurance is left to beneficiaries income tax–free: they receive 100 percent of the benefit.

It can allow you to make a charitable gift of an asset for tax reasons and then act as a replacement for that item to your beneficiaries. It can be used to equalize estates among those who want cash and those who want property.

It allows you to leverage dollars for hundreds, maybe thousands of dollars that create an instant estate for your family. When you were younger, you may have used it to guard against something happening to you, to replace your income. In estate planning it is used to replace money used to pay taxes and expenses, and when used with a pension, it replaces income.

- Don't be too quick to cancel those old life insurance policies.

- Tally them up and see how much benefit you have.

- Do you have insurance that will cover you when you leave your job, or will it end when you leave?

- What liabilities will you have at your death?

Remember, life insurance is not available to everyone; you must be insurable to qualify for it. It is best purchased when you are young and in good health. If you decide to purchase it later in life—be prepared for higher costs and tougher underwriting.

WORKSHEET

Does your estate provide liquidity to cover taxes and expenses or will it be necessary to sell or liquidate assets?

6

NOW THAT I HAVE YOUR ATTENTION

Go for It!

I t's a Sunday afternoon in November. I am finishing up *Retirement Readiness* and I'm also watching a football game. There are two teams, both made up of experts at their positions. Before they went on the field, they did their homework. They practiced, researched the other team, reviewed their strengths and weaknesses, and developed a plan to use them to their advantage. If the plan doesn't go the way they want, they have alternative strategies. They built flexibility into their game. They communicate on the field. Each player needs to know what his teammates are doing. Their game is based on their style, their strengths, and their personnel.

Their goal is to get the ball in the endzone 100 yards away. They are approaching their goal not with long bombs that have a high probability of failure but they are moving down the field with short gains. Five yards, three yards, reassess the situation, then move again. Ball control and field position is the strategy they are using to get to their goal.

This is what I want you to get from this book. As you get close to retirement, I want you to put together a plan and communicate with your mate. Understand what issues apply and what decisions have to be made and how they will affect your lives. Create alternative plans to handle the unexpected. Surround yourself with trusted experts to provide advice when needed.

This book is not about sophisticated strategies. In fact, the examples are the simplest variations of concepts. But it's important for you to understand what you need to prepare for, and how you'll prepare for it based on your goals and needs. Don't take Social Security at sixty-two because your neighbor did; do it because you understand the options, how this decision fits into your plan and how it will benefit you.

The next twenty, thirty, or even forty years will be when you create your definition of retirement and then you live it. Understand the decisions you'll have to make and live the life you want to live before it happens. You're going to be far too busy living and loving life later.

About the Author

M ike Bonacorsi is a CERTIFIED FINANCIAL PLANNER™ professional, author, and public speaker. He is a current member of the Financial Planning Association. He has a unique style, using humor combined with sound financial advice, that is effective with clients from all walks of life. He lives an active life, with golf and ballroom dancing as two of his interests, in Nashua, New Hampshire.